GW00730205

OMO

CHANGE IN
THE VALLEY

MATILDA TEMPERLEY

BURROWHILLBOOKS

BURROWHILLBOOKS

Burrow Hill Books,
Pass Vale Farm, Burrow Hill,
Kingsbury Episcopi,
Martock, Somerset, TA12 6BU
www.matildatemperley.com

Edition 1
ISBN: 978-0-9929401-1-9

A catalogue reference for this book is in the British Library

Author: Matilda Temperley
Images: Matilda Temperley
Graphic Design: Lara Stower at Sibling And Rival

Printed and bound by
EBS – Editoriale Bortolazzi Stei srl
Via Monte Comun 40
37057 San Giovanni Lupatoto
Verona
Italy

ISBN 978-0-9929401-1-9

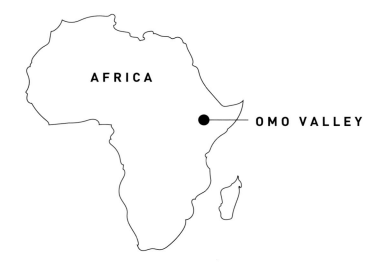

AFRICA

OMO VALLEY

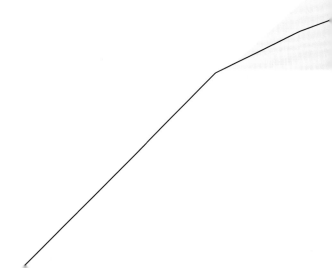

THE OMO VALLEY

TRIBES

• Towns

THE GILGEL GIBE III DAM ●

BODI

● ——— **OMO RIVER**

MURSI

Jinka •

SURI

ETHIOPIA

OUTH
UDAN

Kibish

NYANGATOM

KARA

Kangatin

Dimeka •

Turmi •

ILEMI TRIANGLE
(DISPUTED TERRITORY)

Omorate

DASSENECH

HAMAR

TURKANA

DASSENECH

KENYA

LAKE
TURKANA

TURKANA
SAMBURU
↓

CHANGE IN THE OMO VALLEY AND THE LAKE TURKANA BASIN
2006-2015

In 2006, on my last assignment to East Africa for the London School of Tropical Medicine, I heard whispers of an area in Ethiopia untouched by the modern world. With some weeks to spare from researching the economics of malaria prevention I first visited the Omo valley in south-west Ethiopia in 2007. Far from being untouched by the modern world I found the Omo Valley to be at the forefront of a global movement towards industrialised farming.

In 2006, work began on a hydroelectric dam upstream of the Omo Valley's arterial river and with it came the potential for irrigated agriculture downstream. I have since witnessed a change in the landscape and the people of the Omo Valley. While modernisation is inevitable, in the Omo it appears to be at the expense of the inhabitants rather than at their hands. The scars are visible in the hundreds of thousands of acres of bare earth waiting to be planted by multinational corporations.

SURI

Approximately 40,000 semi-nomadic Suri live to the west of the Omo River in south-west Ethiopia. Life for the Suri revolves around their herds of cattle. Their pastoralist livelihoods are supplemented by rain-dependent cultivation of their staple foods sorghum and maize as well as hunting and gathering. Since the 1980s the Suri have also supplemented their income by panning for alluvial gold in the southern tributaries of the Akobo River.

Niyoyo, Natu, Nacoshi and Nahagani, 2015

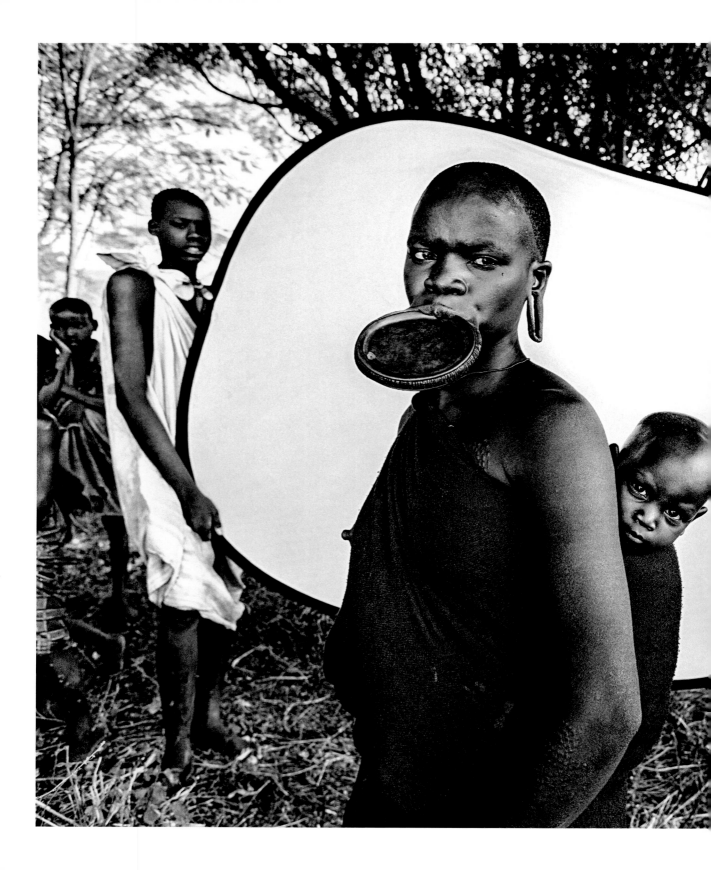

Suri women are renowned for wearing lip plates. A girl's lower lip is cut around puberty. The hole is initially held open by a wooden plug and over time progressively bigger plates stretch it. Lip plates are an expression of adulthood and beauty.

Nasadi and child, 2015

Because the men like lip plates I will
do it myself next year for my husband.
Suri girl, 2015

Suri family, Kibish Town, 2010

The government are stopping the lip plating as they consider it a bad cultural practice and in the last five years it has decreased. The lips are plated much more in remote villages.
Suri man, 2015

Suri Woman, Kibish 2010

Larger lip plates are considered more beautiful. It is often said that the larger the girl's lip plate, the higher the bride price a groom's family must pay. However, many marriages have been pre-arranged and the bride price decided before lip plating starts. In reality, it's up to the girl to decide the size of her lip plate.

Suri woman with wooden plate, Kibish 2010
Suri women make their lip plates from clay decorated with ochre and charcoal. Wood may also be used to make lip plates but it is less common.

Overleaf: **Naguna 2015 and Suri girl, 2010**

We did not dress like this in the past, we
had cow skins like you see in the village.
Slowly, the government is coming here
and they are giving us clothes so this is
changing.

Suri woman, 2015

Suri woman, 2010

Overleaf: **Suri women, 2010**

Before is not like now, there were no schools or Abashhar people [Amharic speakers from the north] so when people didn't have a lip plate, you could see they were from somewhere else. I wanted to cut my lip to be Suri.
Suri woman, 2015

Suri woman, Kibish, 2010

Previous page: **Suri women and children, 2010**

The studio in Kibish, 2015

Our land is near the mountains and when I was young the big lip plates were cut and the women were beautiful and you wanted to immediately pay her family with thirty cattle and one Kalashnikov. Now this [lip plating practice] goes down and down.

Suri man, 2015

Naguna, Kibish, 2015

Overleaf: **Nahagani, Nacoshi, Niyoyo, and Natu, 2015**

Stick fights known as Dongas are an important part of Suri culture. The tournaments begin at the start of the rainy season and continue for three months. This combat sport is fought in heats until only two finalists are left. The winner of a fight will knock his opponent to the ground. While injuries are common, to cause death is strictly forbidden. The Ethiopian authorities have unsuccessfully tried to prohibit the Donga on the grounds of it being 'too violent.'

Kibish Donga, 2010

Previous page: **Suri women, 2015 and 2010**

I have stopped fighting the Donga because I went to school and got an education, but it's in our culture so it doesn't mean other people will stop. It is like a game for us. Its like Wayne Rooney when he plays football – it's the same here, the girls watch us and we become like heroes.

Suri man, 2015

Arriving at the Donga, Kibish, 2010

The Donga can't stop because if we don't fight our fathers won't give us any cattle to marry and the girls won't choose us.

Suri man, 2015

The Donga, 2010

Previous page and overleaf: **Kibish, 2010**

Three years ago I was a student and I was living in the village and fighting Donga and staying at the cattle camp, now I have moved to the town and don't fight.
Suri man, 2015

Fighters at the Donga, 2010

A symbol of wealth, cows are central to Suri life. They provide sustenance, clothes and meat as well as being a link with the spirit world through sacrifice. The small town of Kibish is the capital of the Suri district. New roads to the area are unfurling, opening trade and business routes to both the Ethiopian highlanders and foreign investors. With traditional grazing grounds being confiscated to make way for commercial farms, traditional livelihoods are under-threat. A generation of Suris risk finding themselves with no skills to offer the new market place. The movement of the nomadic Suri into new permanent settlements has been plagued with controversy and reports of human rights abuses.

Kibish River, 2015

What else is there to spend money on? If we are not in the fields we come here and drink.
Suri woman 2015

Kibish town, 2015

Overleaf: **Bars in Kibish town, 2015**

As global prices of fuel and food continue to rise, so too does the incidence of a relatively new phenomenon known as 'land grabbing.' Foreign and domestic investors alike are eager to pour money into countries with lax regulations and ambiguous land use rights... The Ethiopian government, under the guise of promoting free market policies, is ignoring the long-established communal land use rights in order to lease land and water rights to foreign investors.

Emily Ingebretsen, 2012[1]

Mungelo, Nacombole and Baranar in the new village of Regiya Two, 2015

Previous page: **Drinking in Kibish, 2015**
Suri policemen Barcomoro and Leo with Nachulka. In recent years there has been an increase in the number of Suri in local police forces around Kibish.

In the government's settlement program, there is concern that in the new villages there is not sufficient land allowance for the Suri's cattle.

Blood letting, Barguba village, 2015
Village life for the Suri is largely communal. Blood for drinking is drawn by piercing the cow's jugular with an arrow before filling a calabash. Covering it with wet mud closes the wound.

We are not beggars, we just want to be left in peace with our cows. We drink their blood and milk and soon we will not be able to have enough to survive.

Suri man[2]

Milking in Bargula Village, 2015

Overleaf: **Basu in Coca School, 2015**

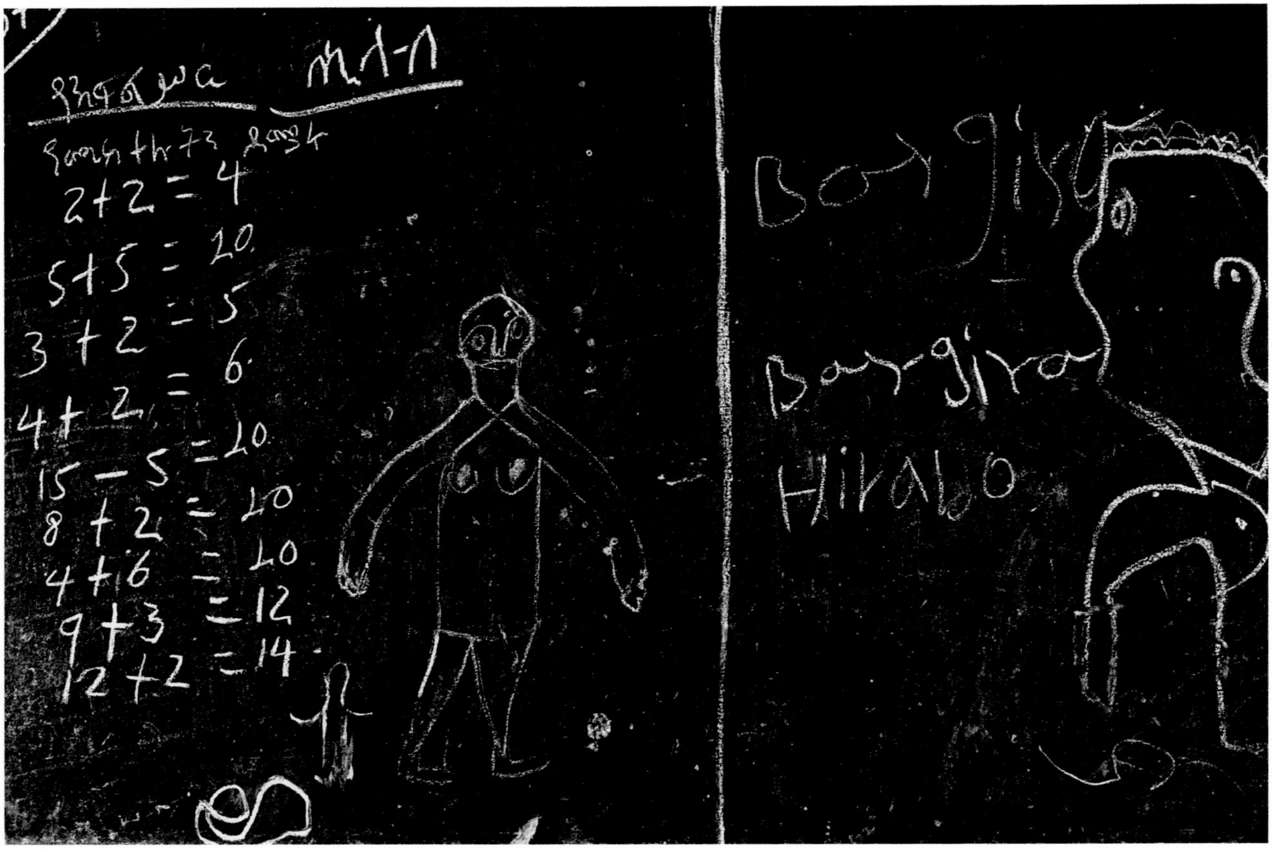
2+2 = 4
5+5 = 10
3+2 = 5
15 − 5 = 10
9+3 = 12
12+2 = 14
Hirabo

Although the Suri are not yet subject to as many tourists as the neighbouring Mursi, it is poignant that the local guides describe those in the most-visited villages as 'looking like the Mursi' in finery which is exotic to both us and to them. Although Suri children commonly paint their bodies with chalk, tourism is changing their style.

Barcoshi and Barcoli, 2015

Some tourists order the painting
and tell us what colours to paint.
Someone said paint half your face
white and yellow, someone asked
the men to paint their whole bodies,
some said paint small patterns.
Suri boy, 2015

**Barsune, Barsue, Bargon, Bargoga, Bardossa,
Barcutel, Tutugo, Barcutel and Bardesho, 2015**

Before the tourists, girls only painted their face during weddings and ceremonies but now there are more and more tourists, there is more painting because the tourists tell them to. For me, sometimes I do this with the kids for money but it's not our culture so it's not good. When the tourists go we wash our faces and go to the town.

Suri woman, 2015

Lanjou, Goguri, Natere and Nakaman in Regiya, the Suri's most touristic village, 2015

When we know tourists are coming, people are waiting in the village to paint themselves. Sometimes the tourists come and say do it like this and so we are always learning what they want.

Suri man, 2015

Nakaman, 2015

MURSI

Less than 10,000 semi-nomadic Mursi live to the east of the Omo River. Like the Suri, the Mursi are agro-pastoralists, herding cattle and goats and cultivating maize and sorghum. During the dry season, they migrate to the banks of the Omo and during the wet season they live in the savannah to the east. The Ethiopian government's Kuraz sugar development encroaches on the Mursi's ancestral lands, threatening both their cultivation and herding practices.

The Ethiopian government is undertaking major industrial development projects in the South Omo Valley that are likely to have important implications for the human rights of the area's inhabitants, particularly its indigenous populations. These include the Gibe III dam project, a 245,000-hectare state-run irrigated sugar plantation, 100,000 hectares of private commercial agriculture, major road infrastructure and oil exploration.

Human Rights Watch 2012 [3]

Mursi woman, 2011

They come every day as long as it is not raining [when the road is bad]; four or five cars usually; 20 to 60 soldiers. They say 'We need this place for sugar [pointing to the surrounding area], so you should not be there. You stay in this place only.'

'What do you think about sugar?' We say 'We don't know,' or 'We don't want it,' but that is not the right answer. They hit us or they take us to jail.

Mursi man, 2011[4]

Mursi woman and child, 2013

Overleaf: **Achuba, 2009 and 2013**

This is a new issue for our people. I have the strong feeling it will be bad. If highlanders are resettled here to provide farm labour there will be drinking, we will slowly sell our cattle, then begging is next. We will lose our self-sufficiency. Our culture will go when the highlanders come. This is the end of pastoralism in southern Ethiopia.

Local official[5]

Mursi woman, 2011

What am I going to eat? They said to take all my cattle and to sell them and to only tie one up at my house. What can I do with only one? I am a Mursi. If hunger comes I bleed a cow's neck and drink blood. If we sell them all for money how will we eat? When we get married we marry with cattle. What will we marry with? What will we eat? When hunger comes what will we feed our children with? If we just keep chickens will we eat soup or milk them?

'This land is my land,' say the highland Ethiopians. 'Run to the forest like a baboon.'

Mursi man[6]

Mursi village, 2013

Since the 1980s automatic rifles have become common in the Omo Valley. They are now the weapons of choice for cattle raids. Efforts at peacemaking between different ethnic groups are increasingly successful but tensions are still high and war breaks out over guns, cattle and girls.

Mursi woman, 2011

Overleaf: **Mursi women, 2011**

Gabinesh, 2013

Overleaf: **Mursi girls, 2009**

The Mursi have become accustomed to tourists descending on their villages every day. At first light convoys of tourists roll into the Mursi villages that are closest to the small town of Jinka. For a moment all is quiet as the women disappear into their homes. A few minutes later they return, their heads adorned with saucepans, belts and baskets. Now, rather than painting themselves in a traditional manner, they are more likely to elaborate their paintwork in an attempt to earn money for pictures.

Mursi woman, 2010

Previous page: **Mursi girls, 2010**

They shot at the tourist car out of exasperation [a two car convoy was shot at in Mursi territory in late 2014]. It is tourism, the land take-over and the sugar factory – all these things contribute to the anger.
Ethiopian guide, 2015

Mursi woman and child, 2011

CHANGE IN THE OMO VALLEY

MATILDA TEMPERLEY

JOANNA EEDE

The Omo River rises on the mountainous plateau of Ethiopia's Shewan Highlands, then flows for hundreds of kilometres through lush grasslands, acacia plains and riverine forests until it reaches Kenya's Lake Turkana. The river's lower valley in the south-west corner of the country is a wild, beautiful, remote region. In the mud and volcanic rock of the Omo's banks palaeontologists have found the fossilised remnants of early hominids, discoveries that have contributed to man's understanding of human evolution.

The Lower Omo Valley is a region where migrating peoples with a broad genetic and linguistic diversity have converged for thousands of years. Today, herdsmen, agro-pastoralists and fishermen live along the lower reaches of the river. Many depend on the flood cycles of the Omo for their survival. Every year the Omo swells, overflows, and deposits silt on the riverbanks as it retreats. It is on this rich, fertile soil that crops such as sorghum, corn, maize and beans have long been planted.

Matilda Temperley's 'Omo – Change In The Valley' is a collection of sensitive and strikingly composed images that are not only testament to the beauty and diversity of the Omo peoples, but a reminder that there are many different ways of being human. Matilda's photographs also show the grim reality of what is happening to their ancestral lands. As she describes in this book, the construction of hydroelectric dam 'Gibe III' will limit the flow of water to the south-western area of the Omo River, so threatening the region's ecology, wildlife and the tribes' flood recession techniques. A program of enforced resettlement is also underway. To make way for the industrial plantations of multinational corporations, the valley's inhabitants are being moved from their lands by the Ethiopian government.

This, tragically, is the story of indigenous peoples the world over. When tribal peoples lose their homelands – be it bush, prairies, sea-ice, mountains, taiga or rainforest – so the fabric of their lives unravels. Lands are their livelihoods, the burial grounds of their ancestors, the source of their spiritual solace, the history of their people and the future of their children. They are still intimately connected to their lands in subtle and complex ways that have long been forgotten elsewhere. So it is no coincidence that tribal peoples who have been separated from their homes – the Innu of Canada, the Bushmen of South Africa, the Australian Aborigines – have been ravaged by catastrophic problems: alcoholism, depression, suicide and chronic diseases.

As an author and writer about indigenous peoples, I am reminded of a time in Tanzania, when one bright dawn I sat with Hadza hunters on a rocky outcrop in Yaeda Chini, north-west Tanzania. 'This is my home,' one of the men said, looking out over the acacia woodland below, deep green from the recent rains. 'Our grandparents lived here' he continued. 'I am part of the land. Without the land, there is no life.'

The cultural heritage in the area that encompasses the Omo Valley and Kenya's neighbouring Lake Turkana Basin has, until recently, been relatively untouched by globalisation. As the result of being a crossroads of human migration for thousands of years, the Omo Valley has a marked diversity of people. At least ten distinct ethnic groups occupy the borders between Kenya, South Sudan and Ethiopia. Like most photographers I was drawn to the Omo Valley not by its landscape but by these inhabitants. The ochre-skinned Hamar, the lip plated Suri and Mursi, and the painted Kara amongst them. While goats and cattle still snake across dirt roads with their attendant children casually carrying Kalashnikovs, the area is no longer a forgotten backwater. The urbanising, industrialising Ethiopian government has placed this valley at the heart of an international agricultural push.

Since my first visit to the Omo Valley in 2007, I have witnessed a change in both the landscape and its inhabitants. While modernisation is inevitable, in the Omo it appears to be at the expense of the inhabitants rather than at their hands. The scars are visible in the hundreds of thousands of acres of bare earth waiting to be planted by multinational corporations.

The fate of the Omo Valley was sealed in 2006 when, upstream of the valley's arterial Omo river, the Ethiopian government began constructing the 'Pride of Ethiopia': the highly ambitious and controversial Gibe III hydroelectric dam. As well as allowing for large-scale commercial farming through irrigated agriculture, Gibe III stands to make Ethiopia a major energy exporter. Since its inception the dam has been controversial. In 2009, the World Bank was forced to withdraw its support because the major contractors were sourced without a competitive tender with 'systematic bias' being cited.[7]

Gibe III has been described as a potential humanitarian disaster for the estimated 500,000 people who live along the Omo River and around its terminal Lake Turkana.[8] The potential outcomes of the dam have also been likened to one of the world's worst ecological disasters; the shrinking of the Aral Sea.[9] This is because the agriculture associated with the dam is expected to considerably decrease the river flow and therefore the volume of Kenya's Lake Turkana, the largest desert lake in the world. In addition, the increase in lake salinity and the decrease in the nutrient-rich annual floods are likely to cause food shortages which will increase the risk of armed inter-ethnic conflict over grazing land.[10] Because changing weather patterns often cause drought and starvation, it is clear that even a small change in the environment could have catastrophic impacts here. When I last visited the lake in 2013, I woke in the morning to find a dead cow at the entrance to my tent – starved to death. The owner was unsuccessfully struggling to get the next bovine victim on her feet. He shrugged when asked and said, 'the floods have not yet arrived, this is normal.'

The government's stance in the face of criticism over Gibe III's social and environmental impact is to accuse its detractors of 'patronising the national interests of Ethiopia and romanticising traditional valley lifestyles.' When in the north of the country, I am often told that 'some sacrifices have to be made for development', especially in a country with exponential population growth where food insecurity is part of everyday life. Trade-offs in a developing nation are inevitable, but in removing the right to self-determination for the hundreds of thousands of people affected by the dam, the Ethiopian government is abusing a basic human right set down by the charter of the United Nations.[11] Because the inhabitants of the Omo Valley have no coherent voice, challenging the government is impossible. This is due not only to the constraints on the freedom of speech in Ethiopia, but also because of ongoing inter-ethnic conflicts and a lack of formal education.

Signs of increasing development are now commonplace. In 2011, I witnessed convoys of heavy machinery carving roads through the mountainsides of the Mago National Park, forging access to the new sugar plantations and factories in Hanna Mursi. I was turned away by the military before I could reach a new sugar factory there, unsurprising given that the Bodi who previously lived on this land had already been almost completely displaced. On this trip, attempts at conversation with the Bodi were met with blank stares and names were withheld. Discussing new farms and factories with foreigners is dangerous for the people in the Omo. This was formalised in 2013 when non-disclosure agreements were established at both the federal and the local level. In recent years my companions in the Omo have often reiterated the fact that for me to mention sugar or dams in public would put them at risk.

One of many new multinational plantations lies alongside the Suri town of Coca. In 2010, the Ethiopian government leased 31,000 hectares of the Suri's traditional dry season rangelands to a Malaysian corporation for palm oil production. Although plans are in place to expand the plantation to 60,000 hectares, the farm is temporarily closed because of security concerns brought about by Suri retaliations. The army is now resident. The government's argument that the plantations will create jobs is persuasive. However it will be economic migrants from central Ethiopia who benefit from the employment and not the local Suri. In a moment of candour, a local trader expressed his fears: 'We are all scared for the future, what if the Chinese own all?' As Ethiopia is at the forefront of an international scramble for African resources, these concerns are well-grounded. Foreign nationals are moving in and a Chinese company has bought the rights to the gold in the artisanal mines along the Akobo River.

In excess of 1,450 square miles are destined for sugar and other mono-crops in the government's drive to move from an economy based on subsistence agriculture, to one of large-scale industrial farming. Until recently, these areas were grazing grounds sustaining the herds of cattle and goats that make up the traditional economy of the Omo Valley. To free this land from its inhabitants, the government brought in the military to move rural families into new villages. In southern Ethiopia, the enforced resettlement or in the case of the nomadic communities, the settlement of an estimated 260,000 people is ongoing.[12]

In Coca, I witnessed the effects of the Ethiopian government's policy of 'villagisation'. A largely empty school sits at the entrance to the town, tin roofs replace traditional earthen thatched houses and soldiers loiter in the streets. In the settlement program, there is concern that there is neither sufficient land allowance for the Suri's cattle herds, nor for their subsistence agriculture. Without the cultural identity that land and livestock provides, the fabric of their pastoralist society is being destroyed. This low-grade, culturally transformative urbanisation is non-negotiable, and villagisation has come with many reports of human rights abuses.[13] The Suri warriors are being turned into beggars, living on food handouts. Human Rights Watch and Oakland Institute have accused the UK and USA's departments for international development (DFID and USAID respectively), of turning a blind eye to evidence of abuse and coercion presented to them. Villagisation is fuelled in part by their donations and through their silence, they are accomplices to these human rights abuses.[14]

I visited the Suri to the West of the Omo earlier this year and the fear fostered by the Ethiopian People's Revolutionary Democratic Front (EPRDF) was palpable. Ironically, while actively eroding the cultural norms, the government simultaneously promotes the Suri as an 'unspoilt tribe.' The Suri receive less than 1000 visitors a year, mostly photographers and filmmakers hoping for a more 'authentic' experience. However, in reality there is little authenticity in a visit to the most popular of the Suri villages. When I entered Regiya, it was impossible not to be struck with guilt at being a participant in the performance that followed. The Suri women renowned for their ceramic and wooden lip plates rushed to collect face paint at first sight of me. Unsolicited, plastic bottles were put aside and t-shirts removed. Children formed tableaux along the path, shimmying up trees to look dreamily into the distance. A huddle of toddlers joined the parade, lying belly-up in the long grass. In the pursuit of 'photo money,' women piled pots, pans, horns and bushes onto their heads; flowers were placed in mouths, stuck in ears and onto nipples. Children lined the road on their knees and banged their arms in unison whilst singing. Offers to scarify themselves, to form singing groups and to add paint ensued. Susan Sontag's words about the 'predatory nature of the photographic act' resounded.

Traditionally, Suri women do paint their faces – but only with white paint and only for weddings. The fancy dress parade I witnessed in Regiya fuels fantasies of exoticism but is performed solely for the benefit of the tourist who pays for the privilege of photographing it. I asked about the lack of mutual curiosity, Naterre, a former Suri spokeswoman, replied wryly, 'this is just for business. We do it for tourists because they ask us to, when the tourists leave we wash our faces and go to the town.'

Hans Silvester's book on tribal decorations 'Natural Fashion: Tribal Decoration from Africa,' made waves in 2009 and might be one reason why outfits in the touristic villages have become more elaborate in recent years. A tide of photographers followed this book and local guides are often expected to provide replications of the images, from the face paint to the foliage. Another Suri woman, Nagullu, voiced concern about the implications for her children, 'When our daughters want to paint their faces for the tourists we must teach them it's not our culture. We only paint our faces like this for money.'

On the other side of the valley, dressing up for tourists has long been normalised. There the tourist dollar is a way of life, and convoys of 4x4s snake into villages, gatecrashing ceremonies and bribing the participants. In 2014, even George W. Bush was amongst the estimated 15,000 visitors to the painted bodies and ceremonies of the Kara, a photogenic ethnic group of some 1,500 people. East of the Omo Valley, popular with tourists, encounters with the lip-plated Mursi women are often described as 'aggressive and uncomfortable.' Having watched a 4x4 convoy arrive in a village at first light, and the ensuing scramble for pictures followed by a hasty retreat twenty minutes later, it is easy to see why. There is no pretence at social interaction. Adding to the objectification of those with lip plates is the fact that it is hard to find a translator and so, for most tourists, it is impossible to breach the little common ground available.

Modernisation of the Omo Valley and Lake Turkana Basin is inevitable and sped up by the construction of the East African super-highway, oil exploration and the tourist dollar. However, the current pace of change driven by the industrial farming practices is impossible for the people of the valley to assimilate. The warring tribes of the Omo Valley, with very little formal education and no cohesive voice are pitted against a repressive government devoid of political pluralism and possessing a single-minded drive for industry.

Five years ago I thought we could be responsible, now it's obvious that people like the Mursi would be happier without tourists. I hate bringing people here now.

Ethiopian guide 2015

Numuri 2013
If a Mursi woman's husband dies she will throw away her lip-plate and unless she is young and without children, it is unlikely she will wear one again.

Previous page: **Sirona and Achuba, 2013**

Overleaf: **Laringi, 2013 and Mursi boy, 2011**

BODI

Approximately 10,000 Bodi live north of the Mursi, practising herding as well as cultivation. In 2011 the Bodi began to be displaced from their ancestral lands to make way for the government's Kuraz sugar plantation. Although the resettlement or 'villagisation' program is described as voluntary, there is no reasonable alternative proposed. Non-disclosure agreements and fear of repression mean that few Bodi are willing to discuss the changes. In the town of Hanna which sits in the centre of the Bodi's land, thousands of labourers from the north have come to work in the new sugar plantation and factory. Ethnic tensions are rife in this rapidly-swelling town.

In the coming five years there will be a very big irrigation project and related agricultural development in this zone. I promise you that even though this area is known as backward in terms of civilisation, it will become an example of rapid development.

Meles Zenawi, Ethiopian Prime Minister, 2011[15]

Mago National Park, 2013
A road is carved through the Mago National Park to service the new sugar factory at Hanna Mursi.

This project violates the rights of indigenous peoples to give free, prior, informed consent to developments on their land, and the rights of indigenous peoples to determine the use of their lands and other resources.

International Rivers Network, 2009[16]

Hanna River, 2013

The government says there is no one here. Where did they go? We have been clearing this land for a very long time. When I was a small girl and I hadn't married yet I was here. My father cultivated here and my grandmother cultivated here. Now I am cultivating here. We grow here like the sorghum. My ancestors died here and I was replanted here like we replant the sorghum seeds. I am here and I am eating from this land. Why is the government saying no one is here and sending the highland Ethiopians here?

Lower Omo Resident [17]

Bodi woman, 2013
Bodi women insert their characteristic chin plugs only after having children. The carved coin-sized plugs have a central spike and are covered in ochre. They represent the woman's achievement as a mother.

Officials made it clear that the government will take most of the land and resettle the population in large villages along the canal — five for the whole Bodi population. They were encouraged to work on the sugar plantations. It was said they would earn 70 birr (US$4) a day.

Lower Omo Resident 2011[18]

Bodi woman, 2013

Arbitrary killings, allegations of torture, beatings, abuse and mistreatment of detainees by security forces, reports of harsh and at times life-threatening prison conditions, arbitrary arrest and detention, infringement of citizens' privacy rights including illegal searches ... allegations of abuses in the implementation of the government's 'villagisation' program, restrictions on academic freedom, restrictions on freedom of assembly, association and movement.

Extract from the US State department's country report on human rights in Ethiopia, 2013 [19]

Bodi women, 2011

NYANGATOM

The Nyangatom live on the south-west of the Omo River. To the north live the Suri and to the east the Kara. The Nyangatom and these neighbouring tribes commonly fight over their scarce resources. Additionally, large farming developments along the Omo River threaten the Nyangatom's grazing grounds and flood recession agriculture.

Loduquo, Kangatin 2013

Overleaf: **Under the mango tree with Epaila, Lochuman, Loqdor and Sockra, 2013**
Nyangatom scarify their faces to establish tribal identity and enhance their appearance. Loqdor's chest scars indicate he has killed a Suri.

We are scared for the future here.
What if the Chinese own all?
Nyangatom man, 2015

Nyangatom woman, 2013

Overleaf: **Nyangatom woman, in Kangatin, 2013**
and newly-wed couple near Kibish, 2010

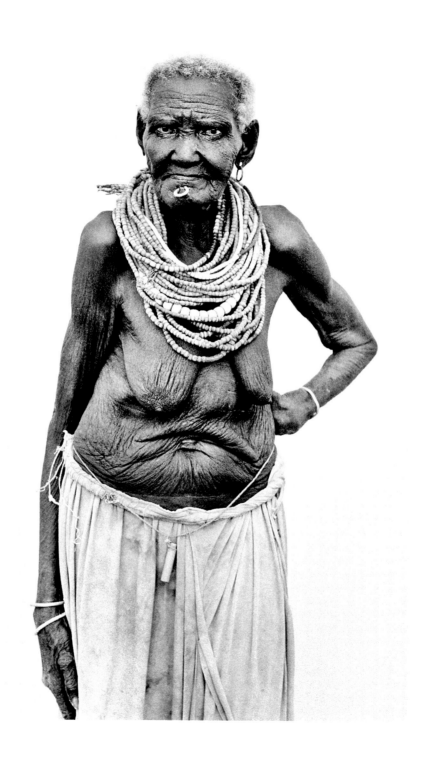

In 2015 a new bridge was built at Kangatin. The bridge spans the Omo River making the remote western bank more accessible. This will allow for future farming developments on Nyangatom land.

The Omo River, 2015

Overleaf: **A new bridge at Kangatin, 2015**

DASSENECH

The Dassenech are agro-pastoralists in the semi-arid region where the Omo River enters Lake Turkana. They rely on flood recession agriculture for survival. Every year the Omo River floods into northern Turkana bringing fertile silt which is essential to renewing the productivity of the land for both pasture and cultivation.

The Dassenech are threatened by ongoing development projects as well as by the government's plans to 'settle' them. The upstream Gibe III hydroelectric dam will regulate the river flow and is expected to decrease the scale and frequency of the annual floods on which their livelihoods depend. In addition, the leasing of traditionally Dassenech land to domestic and international corporations for commercial farming has caused displacement with little or no compensation. In 2013 oil exploration also began on Dassenech land.

Dassenech woman, 2011

Overleaf: **Dassenech girls, 2011**

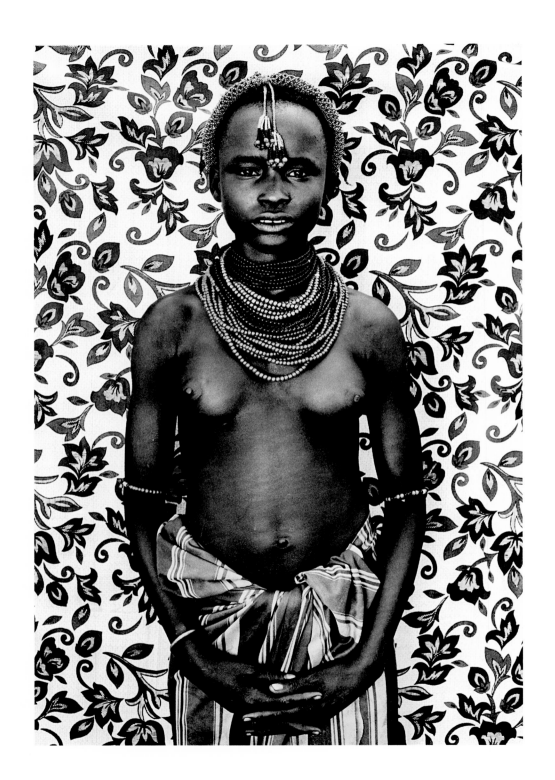

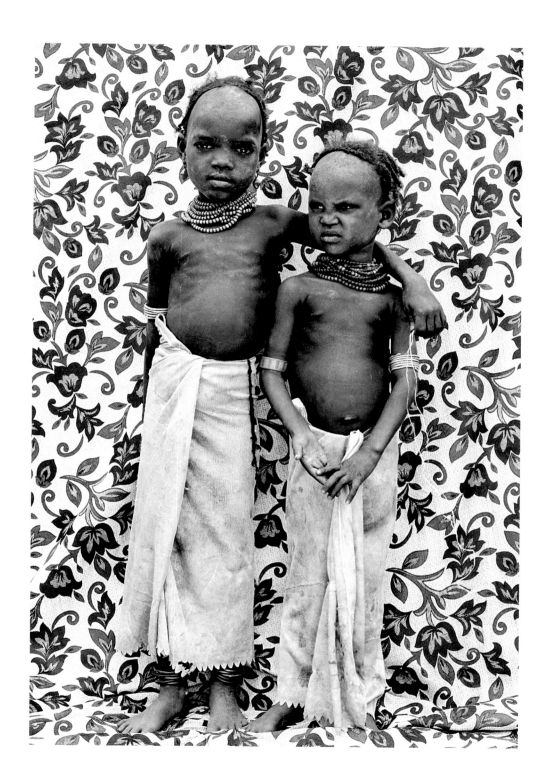

Although the Gibe III and associated irrigation projects claim to provide benefits such as electricity, jobs, and economic benefits for some, the harms they cause will fall squarely on the most vulnerable people in the region.

Catharine Fong, 2014[21]

Dassenech village, 2011

Overleaf: **Lake Turkana fishing camp, 2013**
Traditionally fishing has been frowned upon by the Dassenech and considered an occupation for only the poorest. However it is increasingly being seen as a good income and is important in times of drought when livestock often starve.

Living here is dangerous, but even the Kenyan authorities approve of the presence of the Church on the border with Ethiopia. They hope missionaries can help reconciliation among nomadic tribes.

Father Steven Ochieng 2014[22]

The arrival of missionaries, 2013

KARA

Approximately 1500 Kara live on the eastern bank of the Omo River. The Kara rely on the Omo River's annual flood for flood recession agriculture. This is under threat from the upstream Gibe III hydroelectric dam which will regulate the river flow and is expected to decrease the annual flood. Industrial plantations are also fast displacing the grazing grounds the Kara use for their goats and sheep.

From the escarpment at Korcho village the remote western bank of the Omo River remains green. Below the village, on the more accessible eastern bank, dust storms mark the progress of earth-movers. As far as the eye can see the land is being cleared for a Turkish cotton farm.

Looking west over the Omo River, 2011

The rise and fall of the Omo waters
is the heartbeat of the Lower Omo
Valley. More than any other single
factor, the river determines everyday
economic practice throughout the
region.

Terri Hathaway, International Rivers, 2009[23]

Kara village, 2011

Overleaf: **Kara men, 2009**
Kara are the most decorative of the Omo's inhabitants
painting themselves with white chalk, yellow mineral
rock, pulverised iron ore and black charcoal. Kara men
are permitted to wear a clay hairstyle as an honour for
killing an enemy or dangerous animal.

HAMAR

The Hamar are the Omo Valley's most populous minority. They are described as semi-nomadic although they are more settled than the neighbouring Mursi and Nyangatom. The Hamar are known for their pottery, bee-keeping and metal work. Although they keep cattle, their dry land is most suited to their large herds of goats.

Hamar country is dry, its people are rooks, they are tough. Living between the rocks and drying up, they dig fields and make beehives. That's Hamar.
Baldambe 1975[24]

Hamar man, 2008

Hamar women, 2009

Hamar women put ochre and fat onto their skin and into their hair. Married women wear iron and leather necklaces which are made by the village smiths. The hamar are polygamous but only the first wife wears an upper necklace with an iron protrusion.

Overleaf: **Hamar women, 2013 and 2008**

As the roads have improved, the number of tourists drawn to the Omo Valley has dramatically increased. At the end of the harvest 'bull-jumping' marks a Hamar boy's transition into manhood. Preceding a bull-jump, recent initiates (the *maz*) whip the women of the bull-jumper's family with long switches providing fresh welts to be proudly displayed as declarations of love and loyalty. At dusk, the initiate (the *Ukuli*) must run naked over a line of cattle four times as the *maz* hold them in position. Only after he has achieved this is he considered eligible for marriage.

Preparing for a bull-jumping ceremony, 2013
The *maz* decorate each other while tourists watch.

Previous page: **Hamar woman, 2013 and Arbore woman, 2008**
The Arbore are pastoralists whose territory borders that of the Hamar.

Gathering for a bull-jump, 2013

When our *ukuli* jumps, our girls are whipped by those *maz* whose girls we whipped before. This is the whipping of the girls by the *maz*. They whip, whip, whip.
Baldambe 1975[25]

Hamar women, 2013
Hamar women sing and dance before they engage in the ritual whipping that precedes all bull-jumping ceremonies, 2013.

Overleaf: **Whipping and bull jumping, 2013**
The female family and friends of the bull-jumper provoke the *maz*, begging to be whipped with long switches. The Hamar women proudly exhibit the scars on their backs to show loyalty.

TURKANA

The communities living around Kenya's lake Turkana are mainly nomadic pastoralists herding goats, sheep, camels and donkeys. Lake dwellers also commonly supplement their income by fishing. Although the Turkana are the largest ethnic group, Samburu, Elmolo, Rendille, and Gabra also inhabit the arid shores. Lake Turkana is the world's largest desert lake and the Omo River supplies it with 90% of its water. The Omo River's Gibe III dam and the associated irrigated agriculture in the Lower Omo Valley could lead to a significant drop in Lake Turkana's water level.

In June 2011 UNESCO's World Heritage Committee called for the construction of Ethiopia's Gibe III dam to be halted while the impact on Lake Turkana could be assessed. The potential consequences have been likened to the world's worst ecological disaster: that of the drying up of the Aral Sea.

Lake Turkana, 2011

If completed, Ethiopia's Gibe III Dam will regulate and reduce the Omo River's flow, increasing hunger and fueling conflict throughout the basin... The dam could push Kenya's Lake Turkana – the world's largest desert lake – toward ecological collapse.

International Rivers Network 2009[26]

Turkana woman, Loiyangalani, 2011
Turkana women wear brass or copper chin plugs.

The lake is our heart. When the heart stops beating, there is nothing but death.

Turkana fisherman[27]

Turkana girl, 2011

Overleaf: **Turkana women, 2011**

SAMBURU

The territory of Kenya's semi-nomadic Samburu stretches south from Lake Turkana. If the lake decreases in volume it is expected to lower the groundwater level across the region so that even those living away from the lake shore will be affected. This will lead to an increase in competition for already scarce water resources.

We oppose any current push towards development that is driven predominantly by commercial interest and which undermines our indigenous economies and denies us the little control we have over our already undermined survival.

Lake Turkana's Peoples' Declaration 2009[28]

Samburu woman, 2011

Previous page: **Samburu warrior, 2011**

Overleaf: **Samburu women, 2011**

Cattle rustling between the Turkana and the neighbouring Samburu is commonplace and the conflicts are often violent.

Samburu returning from a cattle raid, 2011

I believe one immediate consequence
(of Gibe III) will be the aggravation of
armed conflict in a war over shrinking
natural resources.
Richard Leakey, 2009[29]

Turkana woman reporting a cattle raid, 2011

[1] **Ingebretsen, Emily 2012,** 'A thirsty third world: How land grabs are leaving Ethiopians in the dust,' 2012

[2] **Oakland Institute 2013,** 'Omo: Local tribes under threat, a field report from the Omo Valley, Ethiopia,' 2013

[3] **Human Rights Watch 2012** 'What Will Happen if Hunger Comes? Abuses against the Indigenous Peoples of Ethiopia's Lower Omo Valley.' Appendix I: Human Rights Watch Letter to the Government of Ethiopia on South Omo, 2012

[4,5,6] **Human Rights Watch 2012,** 'What Will Happen if Hunger Comes? Abuses against the Indigenous Peoples of Ethiopia's Lower Omo Valley.' Human Rights Watch, 2012

[7,8,9,10] **Carr, Claudia 2012,** 'Humanitarian Catastrophe and Regional Armed Conflict Brewing in the Transborder Region of Ethiopia, Kenya and South Sudan: The Proposed Gibe III Dam in Ethiopia.' Africa Resources Working Group 2012
http://www.academia.edu/8385749/Carr_ARWG_Gibe_III_Dam_Report

[11] **United Nations Charter,** http://www.un.org/en/documents/charter/chapter1.shtml

[12,13,14] **Oakland Institute 2013,** 'Understanding Land Investment Deals in Africa – Ignoring Abuse in Ethiopia: DFID and USAID in the Lower Omo Valley,' 2013

[15] **Meles Zenawi, 2011,** Extract from a speech given by the Ethiopian Prime Minister in Jinka, 2011.
http://www.mursi.org/pdf/Meles%20Jinka%20speech.pdf

[16] **International Rivers Network 2009,** 'Ethiopia's Gibe 3 Dam: Sowing Hunger and Conflict,' 2009

[17] **Human Rights Watch 2012, Human Rights Watch 2012,** 'What Will Happen if Hunger Comes? Abuses against the Indigenous Peoples of Ethiopia's Lower Omo Valley.' Human Rights Watch, 2012

[18] **Human rights Watch, 2012** "What Will Happen if Hunger Comes?' Abuses against the Indigenous Peoples of Ethiopia's Lower Omo Valley," June 2012

[19] **US State Department 2013,** 'Country Report on Human Rights Practice: Ethiopia,' Bureau Of Democracy Human Rights, And Labor, 2013

[20] **Corry, Stephen 2010,** Director of Survival International,
https://www.internationalrivers.org/resources/gibe-iii-threatens-world-heritage-sites-3096

[21] **Fong, Catherine, 2014,** 'A Cascade of Development on the Omo River,' 2014

[22] **Ochieng, Father Steven 2014,** 'Extract from an interview by Marie Czernin, 2014'
http://www.southworld.net/kenya-lake-turkana-peace-mission/

[23] **Hathaway, Terri 2009,** 'Facing Gibe 3 Dam: Indigenous Communities of Ethiopia's Lower Omo Valley', International Rivers, January 26, 2009

[24,25] **Strecker, Ivo, Jean Lydall, and P. T. W. Baxter 1984,** 'The Hamar of Southern Ethiopia,' 1984

[26,27] **International Rivers Network 2009,** 'Ethiopia's Gibe 3 Dam: Sowing Hunger and Conflict,' May 2009,

[28] **Lake Turkana' People's Declaration 2009**
http://www.internationalrivers.org/resources/lake-turkana-people%E2%80%99s-declaration-4309

[29] **Leakey, Richard 2009,** 'The Gibe III dam must be stopped,' March 26, 2009
http://richardleakey.wildlifedirect.org/2009/03/26/the-gibe-iii-dam-must-be-stopped/

THANKS

My thanks go for the most part to those people of the Omo Valley and Lake Turkana Basin who have allowed me to photograph them and who have shared their stories with me. They also go to 'Mikey' and 'Chewy' who have encouraged me to love their country. Thanks especially to 'Chewy' who over eight years has taken me on many an adventure, taught me patience and has become one of my greatest friends. Many other people played a vital role in this book, not least the translators and the drivers, the armed escorts and the scouts. Finally thank you to those others who came along for an adventure and who hopefully have fond memories of bumpy roads, guns, breakdowns, illness, earth beds and the endless wielding of reflector pads. This is especially relevant to my mother Diana Temperley whose obsession with anything made of clay, combined with an ability to sleep through gunshots makes her the best travel companion.

Names in the book have been spelled phonetically. To protect their identity, where quotes have been taken from interviews with the author, names have been withheld deliberately. The publisher has made every effort to credit correctly the copyright holder of any additional quotes in this book. We apologise in advance for unintentional omissions and will correct these in future editions.

Matilda Temperley was born in 1981 on her family's cider farm in the shadow of Burrow Hill in the heart of the Somerset Levels. Matilda initially left Somerset to study zoology at Edinburgh University, followed by a Masters degree in the Control of Infectious Diseases at the London School of Hygiene and Tropical Medicine.

While researching the economics of malaria control in East Africa, Matilda discovered a passion for cameras and returned to the UK to carve out a new career.

For her first book 'Under The Surface – Somerset Floods' Matilda won the Royal Photographic Society's Vic Odden Award. Change in the Omo Valley is Matilda's second book. This book is dedicated to the marginalised people of the Omo Valley and Lake Turkana basin.